SCIENCE IN OUR WORLD

STARTING
and
STOPPING

Contributory Author
Brian Knapp, BSc, PhD
Art Director
Duncan McCrae, BSc
Special models
Tim Fulford, MA, Head of Design and Technology,
Leighton Park School
Special photography
Graham Servante
Editorial consultant
Rita Owen
Illustrations
David Hardy and David Woodroffe
Science advisor
Jack Brettle, BSc, PhD, Chief Research Scientist,
Pilkington plc
Print consultants
Landmark Production Consultants Ltd
Printed and bound in Hong Kong
Produced by
EARTHSCAPE EDITIONS

First published in the United Kingdom in 1992
by Atlantic Europe Publishing Company Limited,
86 Peppard Road, Sonning Common, Reading,
Berkshire, RG4 9RP, UK

Copyright © 1992
Atlantic Europe Publishing Company Limited

Publication Data

Knapp, Brian
   Starting and stopping – (Science in our world; 20)
   1. Motion – For children
   I. Title   II. Series
531.11

ISBN 1-869860-76-4

In this book you will find some words that have been shown in **bold** type. There is a full explanation of each of these words on pages 46 and 47.

On many pages you will find experiments that you might like to try for yourself. They have been put in a yellow box like this.

Acknowledgements
The publishers would like to thank the following:
Chris at Mike's Bikes, Leighton Park School,
Micklands County Primary School and
Redlands County Primary School.

Picture credits
t=top b=bottom l=left r=right

All photographs from the Earthscape Editions
photographic library except the following:
David Higgs 7tl, 21, 22, 23; NASA 7tr; Tim Fulford
30l; ZEFA 12/13, 14/15, 26/27, 27t, 31b, 39, 44/45.

Contents

Introduction

Lift up your arm, place your finger on the surface of a table, rub your finger across a table, put your arm down again. In carrying out these actions you did three things, you started, you moved your finger for a time and then you stopped, bringing your hand to rest.

Every time you move you have to start, and eventually you have to stop. To do any of these things you need the power to do some work. In other words you need the **energy** to carry out the movement.

The energy to move your arm or your finger comes from stored energy in your **muscles**. When you rubbed your finger across the table you will also have noticed a resisting **force**, or stickiness. This is called **friction** and it resists every movement you ever make. Friction was also working when

you lifted your arm, because you were pushing air out of the way and moving your muscle fibres across each other.

In some cases it is important to reach a high speed quickly. This is called **acceleration**. Usually acceleration is power-hungry. A cheetah can sprint from rest to 100 kilometres an hour within a few seconds in order to catch its prey, but it soon tires and has to stop.

Stopping quickly (or **deceleration**) means getting rid of power fast and this usually involves making heat. Brakes can burn up if they are used to stop a vehicle too quickly.

In this book you can discover in any way you choose the background behind starting, overcoming friction, accelerating and stopping. Just turn to a page and begin your discoveries.

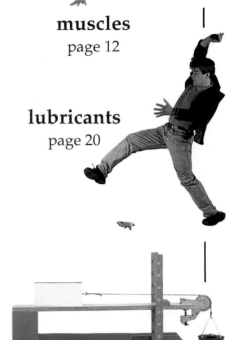

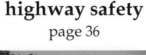

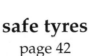

Finding the energy to start

Starting depends on providing a source of energy for movement. On some occasions the source of energy is **stored energy**, that we get from the food we eat, or the petrol that it used by vehicles; on other occasions **movement energy** is shared, such as when a ball is hit with a bat.

Designing for a fast start

The energy to start something moving is often made of many parts. For example, when an athlete jumps on a trampoline several things happen at the same time to give the athlete a huge amount of bouncing energy.

The trampoline is designed to store some of the energy of the athlete's jump and then use it to make the athlete rebound fast. As the feet hit the trampoline the surface fabric stretches and absorbs the energy of the falling person, then it pulls straight quickly. At the same time the athlete bends their knees and braces for the upward movement. By changing shape, the fabric and knees store up energy and then release it very quickly into a spectacular bounce.

(For more information on energy see the book Energy in the Science in our World series.)

One of the most dramatic ways of starting is to take off in a space shuttle powered by a giant space rocket. Solid rocket fuel is one of the most concentrated sources of starting energy, but there are many others

These sand yachts begin to move when the air passing across the sails is at the right speed. In this case the moving wind shares energy with the sails

(For more information on sails, wings and windmills see the book Flight in the Science in our World series.)

Fast hit
As you kick a football look to see the ball change shape before flying away from your foot. Then try to say how a tennis player's swing, the stretch of the racquet strings, and the squashing of the ball as it is hit, all combine to make a tennis ball travel at speeds up to 150 km per hour.

Falling weight mover

All machines work by converting stored energy into movement energy. Sometimes the source of energy might be a supply of electricity (to make an electric motor start turning), or a **fuel** supply such as petroleum (which explodes inside an engine to force pistons up and down). But it is easiest to see the principles of starting by using a machine that more obviously converts stored energy into movement energy.

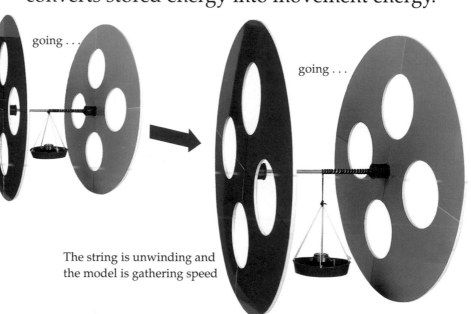

going . . .

going . . .

The string is fully wound and the scale pan is at its highest position

The string is unwinding and the model is gathering speed

Weight-propelled 'wheelie'

The wheelie shown on this page helps you to investigate the way stored (position) energy can be converted into movement energy.

Ask a grown-up to help you to make the wheelie. First cut the wheels from foam board or stiff card. A waste bin makes a good size to use to mark out a circle. Glue cotton reels at the centres of the wheels to make the hubs; leave the wheels until the glue has set. Fix the wheels together using a dowel stick pushed into the centres of the cotton reels.

Put a weight in the scale pan and wind the string round the spindle by pushing the wheelie across the floor. Now let the wheelie go. It will roll forward as the stored energy of the weight gets less, showing that stored energy can be directly converted into movement energy.

You can investigate how well the model starts on different surfaces, how fast it will accelerate, and its top speed.

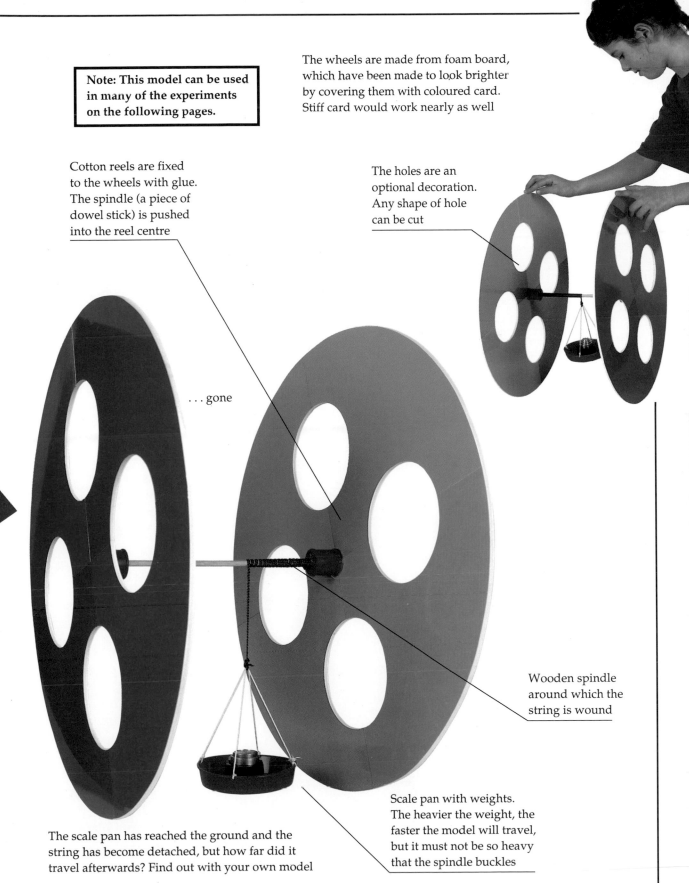

Note: This model can be used
in many of the experiments
on the following pages.

The wheels are made from foam board,
which have been made to look brighter
by covering them with coloured card.
Stiff card would work nearly as well

Cotton reels are fixed
to the wheels with glue.
The spindle (a piece of
dowel stick) is pushed
into the reel centre

The holes are an
optional decoration.
Any shape of hole
can be cut

. . . gone

Wooden spindle
around which the
string is wound

The scale pan has reached the ground and the
string has become detached, but how far did it
travel afterwards? Find out with your own model

Scale pan with weights.
The heavier the weight, the
faster the model will travel,
but it must not be so heavy
that the spindle buckles

Stored energy dragster

Many moving objects get their energy from an on-board store. We get our energy from the food we eat and vehicles get their energy from the **fossil fuel** they use. In the example on this page the energy is stored in a stretched and twisted elastic band. As the elastic tries to untwist it applies a force to the rod. In the case of an elastically-driven propeller, such as you might find on a model aircraft, the rod is made into a blade which begins to spin as soon as it is released. However, in this ground roller or dragster, because the rod cannot spin the roller twists round and round instead.

Note: you can cover the roller with different materials to find out the effects of friction (see page 18).

Use the arm to wind up the elastic

Make a dragster

This simple machine is made from a length of dowel rod, a large elastic band, a length of string and a cardboard tube.

You need to make two discs for the ends of the tube and in each make a hole big enough for the elastic band.

Loop the band through one disc and fix it with a short length of dowel. Thread the string through the hole in the other disc, then through the free loop in the elastic and back through the disc. By pulling the string you can easily stretch the elastic enough to pull it through the disc and let you push the dragster rod through the end. Take the string away and the elastic will hold the machine together.

Wind up the dragster by turning the rod, then place it on the floor and let it go.

Experiment with the number of turns needed to get the dragster going. This will be a measure of the force needed to get the machine to start moving.

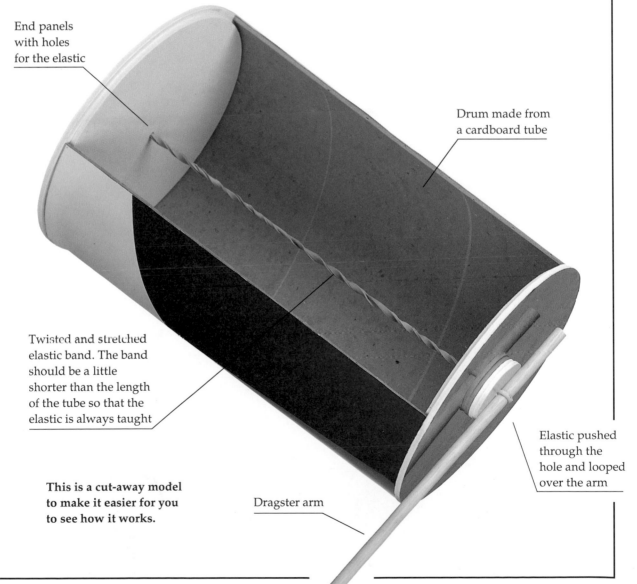

End panels with holes for the elastic

Drum made from a cardboard tube

Twisted and stretched elastic band. The band should be a little shorter than the length of the tube so that the elastic is always taught

Elastic pushed through the hole and looped over the arm

This is a cut-away model to make it easier for you to see how it works.

Dragster arm

11

Starting muscles

When living things want to start moving they change the chemical energy stored in their blood into movement energy. A fast start, however, needs a rapid transfer of energy. This can be achieved by first slowly tightening the muscles.

Feel your muscles

To move quickly from starting blocks, people use many sets of muscles that stretch across the joints in their feet and legs.

The body uses the stored energy in one set of tightened muscles to push against the ground, enabling the body to move.

Feel the muscles stretch and shorten as you bend your legs. There are two sets: one set is to pull the leg straight, and another set is to make the leg bend again. Muscles get stored energy from chemicals such as sugars in food. These are supplied to the muscles through the blood stream.

A frog springs up to catch its prey on a stalk. Its legs contain long muscles which can be tightened almost instantly. This jerks the legs straight and gives the frog a very quick take off

This athlete prepares his leg muscles by bending them before the race begins

Hip joint

Straightening muscle

Bending muscle

Knee joint

Bone

Heel joint

Toe joints

13

Pushing for a start

One of the most important things about starting is to be able to push most effectively against an object like the ground. Then the force from your legs will give you the fastest possible start. Special shoes and starting blocks show the science of forces in action.

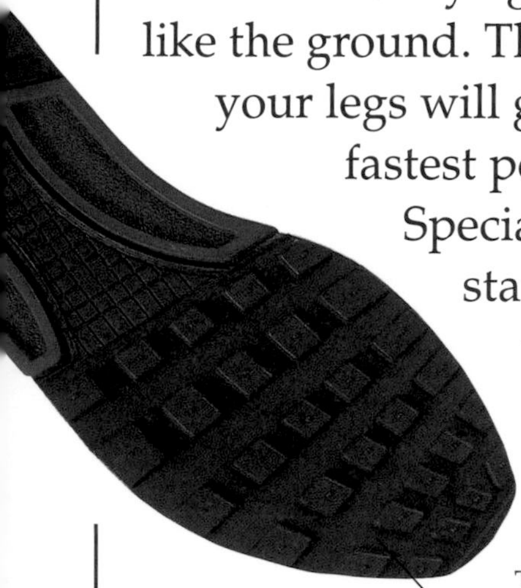

The picture below shows why a good tread near the front of the sole is vital when sprinting

Shoes that do not slip

When athletes begin a race they push backwards with the soles of their shoes. If they push too strongly the force of their push will make their shoes slip on the track.

To help prevent slipping, and therefore wasting energy, running shoes have specially designed gripping soles with a pattern of ridges, or tread, that digs into the ground.

Shoes designed for use on hard smooth surface like a squash court have a flat sole made from slightly sticky material and very few ridges.

Within a few strides the athlete is digging the balls of her feet almost vertically into the track, and shoes with a good tread are enough to stop the risk of slipping

The right angle

Experiment with a pair of starting blocks to find the best angle for a fast start.

First make sure you have the blocks firmly anchored in a track using the securing pins.

Start with the blocks completely flat and see what the result is like. Then angle the blocks a little more each time and test the benefit in getting a good start. You might like to time yourself or a friend over a ten-metre dash.

The best angle of a starting block may vary between people. Can you think why this might be?

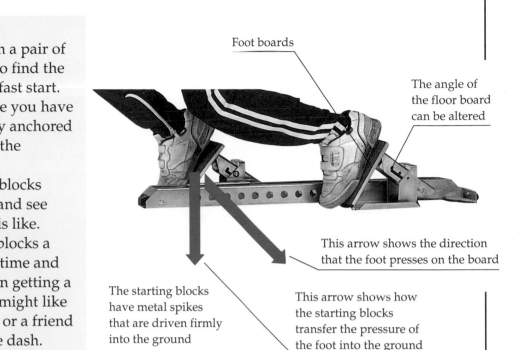

Foot boards

The angle of the floor board can be altered

This arrow shows the direction that the foot presses on the board

The starting blocks have metal spikes that are driven firmly into the ground

This arrow shows how the starting blocks transfer the pressure of the foot into the ground

The picture above shows how the angle of the legs change. At the start the legs are almost horizontal and she needs starting blocks to stop her feet slipping

Gears and levers

Starting is the hardest part in moving.
Many machines, therefore, are designed to
give enough force to get them started,
and then to reduce the force to
keep the movement going.

Lever

Rollers

How to get a starting advantage
You can move a heavy weight a short distance at a time by using a stout bar and levering the weight along, using the ground as a **pivot**.

Even more advantage can be achieved by putting the weight on rollers. However, as the block moves forward, rollers have to be taken from the back and placed ahead of the block. An adaptation of the lever-roller system can be seen on tank tracks.

The giant blocks needed to make Stonehenge, England over 5000 years ago may have been brought over 80 km using the lever and roller system. Both levers and rollers would have been tree trunks. The huge stone heads on Easter Island in the Pacific Ocean were probably moved in the same way

Mobile advantage

A lever and rollers give starting advantage, but they are not easy to use in many situations. This is why many machines have their motors and levers on board. For example, your legs are the motor and levers of a bicycle.

The first bicycles, such as the 'Penny-farthing', had the pedals directly on the front wheel. To get a starting advantage the wheel had to be huge and it was extremely difficult to get on and off the machine.

Soon people found they could have pedals in a more convenient place by attaching the pedals to the wheel through a chain and using **gears**.

The design of the Penny-farthing bicycle did not provide an easy way of starting for the rider, so it was soon discarded. Today Penny-farthings are simply collectable curiosities

Legs, pedals and pedal arms act as a lever

Modern bikes use gears to give starting advantage

Investigate starting advantage

Find out about the advantage of a lever by making the equipment shown on the opposite page. Try changing your grip along the bar to see how the lever effect works.

Then make the gear system shown above. It is made from two cardboard tubes wrapped with corrugated paper and a chain made of more corrugated paper.

Turn the smaller gear and feel the way it pulls on the larger gear. Now turn the larger gear and feel the way it pulls on the smaller. Which way round gives the greater pulling, and therefore starting, power? Check your finding with the gears on the bicycle shown above or on your own bicycle.

Friction

The 'grip' that shoes give us can be used to give a good start when racing. But the grip, a natural stickiness called friction, can also use up most of the energy we put into starting and moving.

This is what friction is, and how we can measure its effect.

There is friction between the wheel and the spindle it turns on

There is friction between the tyre and the brake blocks

There is friction between the tyre and the road

There is friction between the teeth of the gear and the gear wheel

There is friction between the foot and the pedal

Starting and moving friction

Moving friction has a smaller value than starting friction. This is why it is always harder to get a bicycle started than to keep it going.

What affects friction?

Friction is a measure of the roughness of two touching surfaces.

If you place two pieces of sandpaper together, the sand grains on one surface partly fit into the spaces between the sand grains on the other paper. As a result the two pieces of sandpaper are partly locked together and it is difficult to rub one piece over another.

Sandpaper has a high friction because of its obvious coarse bumps and dips. But all surfaces, no matter how smooth they look, have bumps and dips. The fewer the bumps and dips the lower the friction.

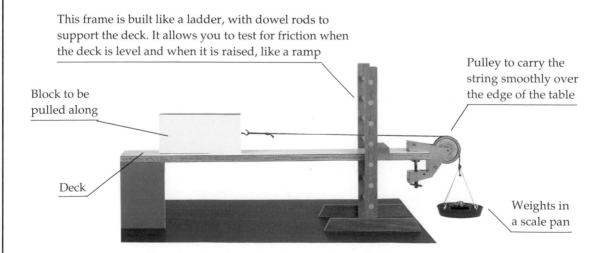

This frame is built like a ladder, with dowel rods to support the deck. It allows you to test for friction when the deck is level and when it is raised, like a ramp

Pulley to carry the string smoothly over the edge of the table

Block to be pulled along

Deck

Weights in a scale pan

Finding out about starting and moving friction

Attach a block of wood to a scale pan using string. Run the string over a pulley fixed to a flat surface (the deck) so that adding weights to the scale pan makes a sideways pull on the block.

Begin by adding small weights to the pan. The block will not move because the friction between the block and the deck is too great.

Keep adding weights and eventually the block will move. Now you have overcome starting friction.

Take off a few weights and give the block a small nudge to get it moving. If it comes to a halt, add weights until the block keeps moving after the nudge. You will find fewer weights are needed to keep the block moving than to start it moving.

Repeating the experiment with the deck raised into a ramp will allow you to find out the effects of slope on movement.

More experiments with your wheelie

You can try the same experiment with your wheelie (see page 8) to find out the weight needed to overcome friction. This part of the stored energy is 'wasted'.

Here you see the deck raised on the frame to make a ramp which can test the effects of slopes

Investigate materials

Find out about the friction of various materials. You can try various grades of sandpaper and any other material that can be fixed to the underside of the block. Double sided adhesive tape is a good material to use for sticking the material to the block.

Reducing friction

Energy has to be used overcoming friction. It is therefore very important to think about ways in which friction can be reduced, and one of the best ways is to use a slippery material – often called a **lubricant**.

Slugs and snails produce a type of slime called **mucus**. It helps them to move easily over the ground

Find out how to make starting easier
Use the block of wood and pulley shown on page 18 to find out about lubricants. Simply smear some lubricant on the underside of the block and then find out how much weight is needed to make the block move.

Investigate water, oil (from an oil can), washing up liquid, soap and petroleum jelly to see which is the most effective.

What is a lubricant?
A lubricant is any material that can be placed between two surfaces to make them move across one another more easily.

A lubricant works by putting a film of slippery material between two surfaces that would otherwise touch. Water is often a good lubricant, but because it runs away easily and readily evaporates, its uses are limited.

Oil and grease make excellent lubricants and are used in many machines. However, there are many other slippery materials, including powdered rocks and minerals such as graphite (the 'lead' in pencils).

This ball bearing cage is packed with grease as a lubricant. Grease is slippy, but because it is also sticky it will not run out of the cage

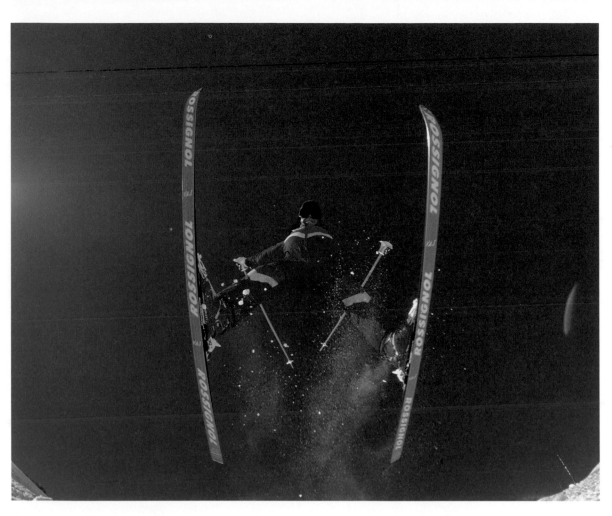

Skis are designed to have as little frictional resistance as possible. They have shiny bottom surfaces that are coated in special lubricants before each use

Find out about friction

If you rub your hands together quickly for a few seconds you will find that they begin to warm up. The heat is produced as friction soaks up some movement energy and turns it into heat.

See what happens when you rub your hands while pressing them together more strongly and then less strongly. You should find that changing the pressure changes the friction.

Now try using wet hands. Does this change the friction? What about adding soap to your hands?

You can experiment with many materials to find out which is the slippiest.

The importance of friction

Friction may be a nuisance when we want to get started, but friction is a very important controlling force. Friction is the gripping force that keeps tyres on a road and brings cars and bicycles to a stop. Friction on ice is very poor, which is just what skiers use to full advantage when they make their spectacular jumps!

What is drag?

When you move quickly through the air you can feel the wind on your face; when you swim through the water you can feel the water being pushed aside.

In both of these cases you can only go forward because you are able to push some of the **fluid** (air or water) out of the way. Drag is the resistance of the fluid to being pushed out of the way.

Design to reduce drag is common. What design features can you see about this train that indicate that it is designed to move at high speeds?

In the picture on the right a new kind of ski helmet is being tested to see how it will help to reduce drag. The lines are smoke trails

The effect of speed

Drag is not an important feature when moving slowly. For example, a snail crawling along a wall, does not have to use much energy to push its way through the air.

But as speed increases, so drag becomes important and special designs have to be used to reduce the amount of energy that would otherwise be used up. In fact it is so important that competition swimmers and cyclists wear special clothes, and vehicles, trains, ships and aircraft are designed to special shapes all to keep down the effect of drag.

This picture shows a downhill skier on a slope. The special suit, the helmet and the standing position, with arms held well in to the body and knees bent were developed from experiments in the wind tunnel. Each enables the skier to go a little faster

Checking for drag

One way to see the amount of drag is to use a wind tunnel and smoke wands. Each smoke wand gives out a long stream of smoke from a very small nozzle. As the smoke is carried through the air its trail picks out the way the air is moving. If there is little drag then the smoke trails will be smooth, but if the drag is severe the smoke trails will be very disturbed.

Check for drag

Look at vehicles in the street to see how they have been designed to reduce drag. Are newer vehicles better designed in this respect than older ones?

Cut out some pictures of vehicles from magazines and paste them on to paper. Mark those places where you think parts stand up awkwardly and draw on the modifications you think would help reduce drag.

Saving fuel

When vehicles move fast they upset the air flow and this causes drag. Aircraft bodies are specially designed to keep drag to a minimum, which is why they are designed in pencil-like shapes. Special shaping to reduce drag is called **streamlining**.

Making a truck into a similar pencil shape would make it very difficult to pack it economically. Nevertheless, even a small amount of streamlining can help to save fuel.

The bodies of trucks are designed around the goods they have to carry. Many cannot be rounded because their job is to carry boxes. This is why only the cab shape is streamlined

This truck has been made with little effort at streamlining because it is used in a country where fuel is still not expensive. Manufacturers only make efforts at streamlining as fuel becomes an important cost for the truck owner

Road shapes

Even an awkward shape like a truck can be streamlined.

The shape of the panel above the drivers cab (called the cowling) can be designed to make the air flow round the truck body smoothly. By using the cowling, trucks can improve their fuel use by over 10 per cent.

Drag racing

Drag racers want to accelerate as fast as possible and everything about the machine is designed to this end.

A drag race may be over in 5 seconds and in this time the machines may have covered half a kilometre – and the drivers will have experienced a gravitational force twice as great as an astronaut taking off in a space rocket!

Engine placed in front of the wheels to help keep the dragster on the ground

Very long body designed simply as a counterweight. The front wheels arc tiny and are used for small direction changes only

Massive wheels with wide tyres designed to give maximum grip. Even so you can see the wheel slip is causing the tyre rubber to heat up and make smoke

Very powerful engine designed to give maximum acceleration. The top speed does not matter

Moving through water

Starting and stopping in water is very different from starting and stopping on land. There is little friction between a body of a fish or the hull of a ship and the water. Fish accelerate and decelerate by flexing their bodies from side to side. By contrast, people have had to design special forms of paddle or screw to push or pull vessels through the water.

Fast-swimming fish

Much of the body of a fish is made of muscle. A fish has red muscle in two strips, one down each sids of its body and white muscle that makes up the main body.

When moving slowly it is the red muscle, with more blood and therefore more oxygen, that is used, contracting first one side then the other to give a sideways movement. However, when the fish needs to accelerate quickly to escape being caught or to catch a prey, it uses the white muscle to give the spurt of speed needed.

Red muscle for cruising at 1 body length per second

White muscles allow a fish to move at 15 body lengths a second. This fast swimming can only be maintained for short periods such as when catching food or when getting out of trouble

When the fish wants to put on a burst of speed it uses the white muscles. This starts as alternating motions down the flanks but by the time the motion has got to the tail the muscles move together to give the tail rigidity

Propellers

A propeller is a set of blades curved in such a way as to act like a screw. As they turn, the blades pull water from ahead of the blades and push it out at the back.

Canoe paddles

Canoe paddles are designed to work in a similar way to a propeller. Each slightly curved blade enters the water with little disturbance.

The flat of the blade pulls the canoe forwards, and the curve on the trailing side of the blade allows the blade to be pulled out of the water smoothly.

Changing speed in the air

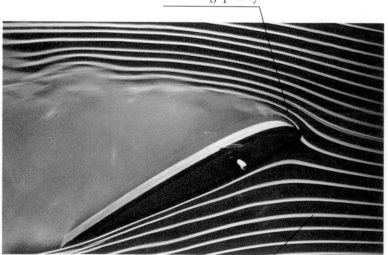

Birds, insects and aircraft are all specifically designed to allow them to take off and land with ease. Many insects beat their wings in such a way that they act just like propellers, and they can start and stop very quickly. Birds and aircraft use their broad wings for gliding, and they change speed by altering the shape of their wings.

(For more information on wings and flying see the book Flight *in the Science in our World series.)*

Closely spaced trails of smoke show where the air is flowing quickly

Design a starting wing
The greatest **lift** is needed during starting. Make this model with a pieces of thin card folded and stuck as shown in the picture above.

Place a straw through the wing and thread it onto thin string. Run forward to find out how fast the wing rises up the string.

Try different designs of wing to get the greatest lifting speed.

Testing a wing for lift
Wings are designed in large wind tunnels with smoke trails to show how the air moves. For a fast lift-off designers aim to get air flowing more quickly above the wing and slower underneath it.

Widely spaced smoke lines show where the air is flowing more slowly

Changing wing shape

Birds are among the masters of the air mainly because they can change the shape and angle of their wings quickly. This gives them power to accelerate, to glide and to stop in amazingly precise ways.

Aircraft can only have fixed wings, but they do have many moveable flaps on their surface, both on the leading (front) edge and on the trailing (rear edge). These flaps are used to change the way the air flows over the wing.

These flaps are used to make the wing less efficient and help it to slow down and lose height

Beating action changes to give 'reversed thrust'

Wing turned to near-stall position

Feet digging into the water to add friction and slow the swan to a halt

Feathers splayed out and curved up (try holding your hand out with splayed fingers to get the same effect)

Laws of Motion

Newton was a famous Scientist who lived over 200 years ago. He discovered the laws that govern starting and stopping. They are called the Laws of Motion.

His first Law of Motion says that a force is needed to make something move, and it is what we have been looking at in the first part of this book.

His second law, and the subject of the last part of the book, says that unless a force is used to slow something down it will carry on moving at the same speed for ever.

Safety in a vehicle

When a driver presses on the brakes of a vehicle the frictional force causes the vehicle to slow down. But the people inside the vehicle do not have brakes, neither do the parcels that may be loose on a rear shelf. Newton's Law predicts that they will continue to move forward until stopped.

This is why there is a real danger that people will be injured by flying parcels if they are not secured and that people will be injured by hitting the windshield if they are not restrained by safety belts.

Pilots in aircraft use safety belts just as drivers of cars

It is common to see standing passengers on a bus or tram lurch backward or forward when the vehicle starts and stops. This is because their feet move with the bus but it takes time for their bodies to catch up!

Merry-go-rounds

A merry-go-round demonstrates the effects of momentum very well. If you begin to spin the machine and stand on it for a while you will reach the same speed as the machine. If you then jump off you will find that you have to run to keep your balance because you have been given momentum by the spinning machine.

Waves travel easily across an ocean because there is too little friction to slow them down. Earthquakes can generate waves called tsunamis which will send water flooding onto coasts thousands of kilometres away from the centre of the earthquake.

Waves only stop when they meet the frictional resistance of a shallow shore

Momentum

Once something is moving it tends to continue moving of its own accord. For example, a truck will continue to move even after the engine has been switched off; a bicycle will carry on moving for a while free-wheeling.

The tendency to carry on moving is called **momentum**. The reason the truck or the bicycle slows down and stops is that friction acts through the brakes, through contact with the road and between all the moving parts of the vehicle.

Test Newton's Law

You can test the effects of Newton's Law for stopping using simple models. The model shown below will help you to understand what happens to a loaded truck (say one filled with milk cartons), while the one opposite imitates what might happen to passengers in a vehicle during an accident if they are not wearing safety belts.

Sliding stopper
You can use the friction machine shown on page 18 to find out what happens when the sliding block hits the pulley.

See what happens when you pile more objects on the block in different combinations and when you put heavier weights in the scale pan. How can this experiment help you to design the safest, most stable kind of load for an open truck?

Take care with flying objects. You should wear safety glasses.

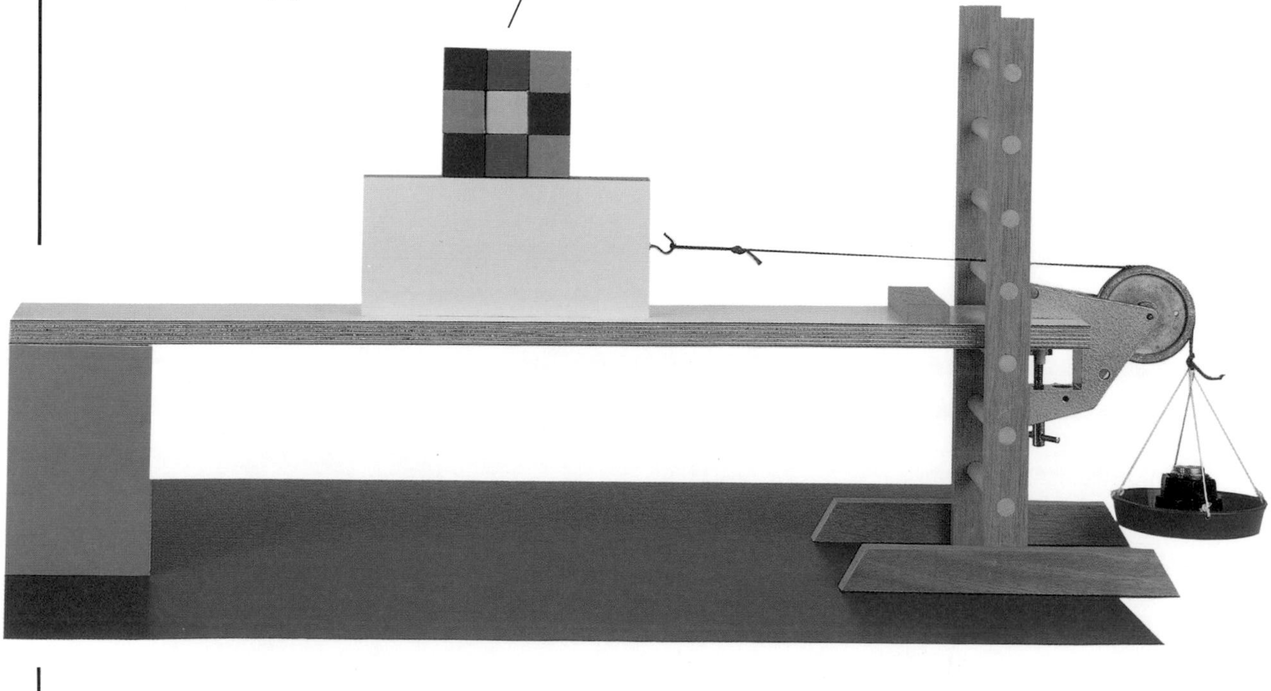

Piled blocks

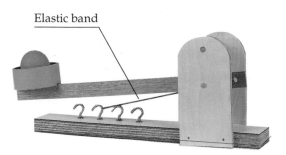
Elastic band

Making a throwing machine
This machine can throw small balls into the air in exactly the same way each time.

You can easily make the one shown in this picture using an elastic band, some pieces of wood and the end of a cardboard tube. You might like to ask a grown-up to help you cut and stick the wooden pieces together.

Cardboard tube

The ball has a light weight and a large volume and it will be slowed down by the air

Fair tests with a throwing machine
The throwing machine is arranged so that when you press down gently on the front edge the ball will be thrown in the air by the machine. This gives a way of testing the effect of speed fairly.

Find out how far a ball will travel by charting the results of the distance thrown against the length the elastic was stretched. Then try it again with a smaller, heavier object like a small wooden ball and an even smaller object like a marble. How can you adapt this model to demonstrate to other people that it makes scientific sense to wear a safety belt?

Rod

(For more ways to use the throwing machine see the book Energy *in the Science in our World series.)*

Wooden base board

Highway safety

Everyone knows that if you ride a bicycle into a wall you will stop immediately – but the consequences can be unpleasant!

If brakes on bicycles, automobiles and trucks were made too fierce, cyclists might risk being thrown over their handlebars and vehicles would run the risk of going out of control.

Safe stopping means we have to control the rate at which we lose movement energy.

What controls stopping distances?

The distance which it takes you to stop depends on: thinking that you must stop; taking action to stop; how fast you are travelling; the weight of your vehicle; how good the brakes are; the condition of the road surface and your tyres.

Charts for stopping

Make a set of bars like the one shown below, but using these figures. Then try pacing out these distances to get a real feeling for the stopping distances involved.

Speed	thinking distance	braking distance	overall distance
80 kph (50 mph)	15 m	38 m	53 m
110 kph (70 mph)	21 m	75 m	96 m

Family automobile travelling at 50 kph (30 mph) (common city speed limit)

Thinking distance 9 m

Vehicle smashes indicate what happens when movement energy cannot be changed in a controlled way

Leaving a safe gap

The faster a vehicle is travelling the longer it will take it to stop. This is the reason why vehicles moving fast on a main highway have to give themselves much longer stopping distances than they would on roads where vehicles travel at slower speeds. They must allow large gaps between themselves and the driver ahead because it will also take some time – and therefore distance – to think and react to someone stopping ahead.

Safety in practice

The cars are travelling along the busy highway shown in the picture below frequently have to slow down because of congestion or because drivers change lanes without looking carefully for overtaking traffic.

Check the picture to see if the faster vehicles are leaving more space than the slower ones. If they are not, what may be the outcome?

Reacting distance 14 m

Overall stopping distance 23 m (nearly 6 vehicle lengths)

Stationary car or potential accident

Skidding to a halt

Skidding is a simple way of slowing down or stopping. When someone intentionally skids they are trying to increase the friction.

Skiers use the braking power of skidding especially as they move quickly downhill by turning their skis at an angle to their path; cyclists skid by turning their front wheel sharply. Motorists can also skid if they push on the brakes so hard that the wheels lock.

Skidding is not used as the normal way of stopping because it is far less controllable than using brakes.

These tyre marks on a road show where the brakes were applied so hard that the wheels locked and the vehicle simply slid forward. Skidding like this is uncontrollable and many accidents happen as the result of skidding

Snow stoppers

Because skis are designed to skim over the surface of the snow, it would take a long time for a skier to come to rest naturally. In downhill skiing there are many obstacles to miss and it is important to be able to stop very quickly indeed when necessary.

To do this the skier turns the skis at right angles to the direction of travel and at the same time turns the leading edge of the skis up and digs the trailing edge into the ground. In this position the blades are very inefficient at skimming the surface.

This skier is throwing up a cloud of snow because the skis have been placed at an angle to the direction in which he is travelling.

Skidding turn

Skidding is useful during racing because the skid can be used to turn a corner without braking. This means a bend can be negotiated much faster than normal.

Skiers throw snow into the air as they skid

Why brakes get hot

If you have ever touched the brakes of a bicycle after hard braking you may have been surprised at just how hot they had become. The brake pads on vehicles have to do a lot of work and they can become so hot that they would burn anyone who touched them.

Finger test

A gyroscope allows you to test the effects of a stopping force. Start the gyroscope and then try to stop it by gripping the spindle of the disc between your fingers.

You should find that it is quite difficult to stop this way. How does this help you to decide where a brake must be applied on a wheel?

Start the gyroscope again and this time try stopping it by rubbing a sharpened pencil lead against the outside of the disc. What happens to the lead, and how quickly does the gyroscope slow down?

Finally start the gyroscope once more and try stopping the disc using the rubber end of a pencil. What are the results like now? Can you find out how to stop the gyroscope smoothly and quickly without it jerking in your hands?

Test the stopping power of brakes

You can test the stopping power of the brakes on your bicycle even at slow speeds.

First chalk a line on the ground on an area where there will not be any traffic.

Use a bicycle that is fitted with a speedometer, cycle to about 10 km an hour and then, when you reach the line, brake smoothly and mark the line where you stop.

Repeat the experiment with just the front brake and then just the rear brake to see which has the most stopping ability.

Carefully increase the pressure on the brakes to try to stop in the shortest possible distance. What problems start to appear? Can you understand why brakes are not made more powerful?

Only use a small gyroscope, no bigger than the one shown in the picture, and ask a grown-up to test the experiment first. Large gyroscopes are extremely powerful and should not be used.

Calliper

Smooth wheel rim
where brakes grip

Brake handle

Connecting
cable

Brake block

Hot brakes!

Brakes are usually small pads
of material that are held close to the
rim of a bicycle wheel. When the brake
handles on the handlebars are squeezed,
cables pull the brake blocks on to the
rims. These are called calliper brakes.

The harder the brake handles are
pulled, the tighter the brake blocks grip
the moving wheel and the faster moving
energy is changed to heat energy.

There is a limit as to how fast the
change can take place, which is the
reason why you do not stop immediately.

Tyres for safe stopping

Two surfaces are needed for stopping: a firm highway surface and a good gripping tyre. Both highways and tyres have to cope with a wide variety of weather conditions. They need to have smooth surfaces for comfortable noise-free driving, but they also have to give good grip in wet weather or there will be a risk of skidding. This is the role of the tread.

This criss-cross pattern is designed to throw water away from the road just as the tyre passes over it. This is only possible if the water can escape along the grooves, or tread of the tyre. This explains why all tyres need a deep tread to be safe in the wet

The pattern allows water to be pushed up between the treads and give the tyre a good grip in the wet

If this depth gets too small, the tyres are nearly worn out and there is a risk of **aquaplaning**

The tyre is filled with air under pressure until it forms the correct shape with the tread flat on the road. This explains why tyres must be inflated to the correct pressure

The way tyres make contact with the ground is most easily seen on a snowy road

Find out how highway surfaces vary

Highways must be designed to shed water during rain and the surfaces must be rough enough to grip the tyres well. At slow speeds even the smooth surface of a house drive gives sufficient grip, but on fast highways a rougher surface is needed to give better stopping power. However, rough surfaces cost more to lay, wear out tyres quickly, and cause increased traffic noise, so they are used only in special areas.

Check to see what the road surfaces are like in your area. Are there special high grip surfaces near road junctions or where pedestrians cross?

The shape of the highway

The easiest way to make water run from the surface of a road is to make it very slightly sloping.

Because wet surfaces are so dangerous, highway often have an inbuilt slope that runs from the middle to the edges (known as the shoulders), this is called the camber. The camber plays a vital part in helping water to run quickly from the highway in wet weather.

In snowy weather normal tyre treads fill up with crushed snow and chains have to be used to get a good grip

The shape of the tyre

Water on a road can be almost as dangerous as oil. A thin film of water can act like a lubricant and a thick film of water is even more dangerous. This is because a fast-moving vehicle tyre may not be able to push the water aside fast enough.

Beyond a certain speed a film of water can remain between the tyre and the road. At this point the driver loses control as the vehicle simply glides over the surface of the water, a phenomenon called aquaplaning.

Tyres have special patterned treads like the one shown on the opposite page, which are designed to push water aside and keep as much rubber as possible firmly on the road.

Racing cars

Racing cars are exciting machines to watch. The drivers may be able to reach speeds of over 300 km per hour and they must be able to start and stop very quickly.

All the lessons of stopping and starting have to be applied to the full in racing machines. Here are some of the things the engineers do.

Rear aerofoil spoilers to catch the air as it blows over the car and push the back wheel down for maximum grip during acceleration

Specially-shaped body panels (cowling) helps force air to cool engine but also reduces body drag

Front aerofoil to make the air split and push the front wheels hard on the ground for maximum steering grip

Very wide wheel base helps to keep the car stable round corners

Wide tyres with no tread for best dry-weather grip. Tyres are changed in wet weather to those with treads on

Pencil-shaped body to give as small air resistance as possible

Very low centre of gravity to make the car as stable as possible. This allows it to go fast round bends without rolling over

New words

acceleration
this is the increase in speed of a body, usually measured in metres per second per second. For an object falling under gravity the acceleration is 9.8 metres per second per second

aquaplaning
the tendency for a thin film of water to develop when a vehicle moves at high speed on a wet road. The purpose of the pattern of deep cuts, or tread, on a tyre is to prevent aquaplaning and loss of control

camber
the slightly arched surface of a road which is designed to provide a slope for water to run off the road during a rainstorm. On curves cambers are often designed with a single slope from the outside towards the inside. This is called banking

deceleration
the reduction in speed of an object. Like acceleration, it is measured in metres per second per second

energy
a property which allows work to be done. The several forms of energy can be converted into each other. Converting stored energy into movement energy is used in starting and moving, whereas converting movement energy into heat energy (through the use of brakes) results in stopping

fluid
the general name for either a liquid or a gas. A fluid will change shape to fit inside a container. Pressure can be transferred through a liquid, and this is used in automobiles when the driver puts a foot on the brake. Liquid is forced along a tube and as it presses against brake pads attached to the other end of the tube, the brakes are applied

force
the agency that changes the speed or the direction of a body. In honour of the scientist Newton, who developed the Laws of Motion, force is measured in units called Newtons

fossil fuel
a source of concentrated stored energy that was produced millions of years ago during the fossilisation of plants and animals. The main fossil fuels and coal, oil and natural gas

friction
the force between two moving bodies that acts as a kind of stickiness, and therefore opposes the motion. The driving force needed to overcome friction for a stationary object is higher than that needed for a moving object, which is why engines must develop their greatest power for starting

fuel
a source of concentrated energy that gives out power when it is burned or changed chemically in some way such as when food is eaten

gears
a set of different sized toothed wheels that interlock in such a way that different amounts of starting advantage can be obtained. During starting, when the greatest advantage is needed, a small wheel on the engine side of the gears is used to drive a large one on the machine

lift
the upward force that is created when a wing moves quickly through the air

lubricant
any substance that will remain between two touching surfaces, helping to fill in the natural dips in a surface and therefore make it easier for two objects to slip past one another

momentum
a property of an object which causes it to keep moving even when the driving force stops. The amount of momentum varies with the speed and the mass of the object, so fast moving, heavy objects have a greater momentum than slow moving lightweight ones

movement energy
otherwise known as kinetic energy, movement energy is gained as stored energy is lost. So, for example, a vehicle moves (has movement energy) so long as it burns a fuel (and therefore loses stored energy)

mucus
a slimy liquid that is released for special glands and which can be used as a lubricant

muscles
the tough, stretchy tissues that surround your bones. Muscles can only shorten (tighten), so two sets of muscles are needed around every joint. A great deal of energy is needed to shorten a muscle. Muscles are under the control of nerves, which is why they can react so quickly

pivot
a short rod or shaft about which an object can revolve

stored energy
otherwise known as potential energy because it has the ability, or potential to do some work. A fuel is a source of stored energy

streamlining
designing the shape of an object to make sure that it pushes air or water aside in a smooth fashion, thereby making the effects of friction as small as possible

Index